AGES 3-5

SCHOLASTIC

PUPPY
Preschool
ACTIVITY BOOK

Editor: Ourania Papacharalambous
Cover design: Tannaz Fassihi
Cover art: Jen Naalchigar
Interior design: Jenny Rez
Interior images: © Shutterstock.com

ISBN 978-1-338-73871-1

3 4 5 6 7 8 9 10   40   26 25 24 23 22

Dear Family,

Does your preschooler have a passion for puppies? Then you have sniffed out the *paws*-itively perfect tool to get him or her excited about learning new skills! At Scholastic, we believe that learning should be joyful and fun, especially for our youngest learners.

Inside this colorful, puppy-themed workbook, you'll find a treasure trove of engaging, skill-building activities developed especially for three- to five-year-olds. Topic areas include:

- Tracing
- Alphabet
- Numbers
- Colors

- Shapes
- Cutting & Pasting
- Basic Concepts
- Fine Motor Skills

We've included lots of activities for your child to complete, plenty of adorable puppy photos to capture his or her attention, and fun stickers as a special reward for a job well done.

So, turn the page and get started today. We hope that you and your child have a delightful time completing these *paw*-some pages!

Sincerely,

The Editors

Safety First! This book contains cut-and-paste activities. Always supervise children when using scissors.

Trace the lines to each puppy's bowl of food.

Puppy Preschool Activity Book

Trace the strings of each puppy's kite.

Trace the waves in the ocean.

Puppy Preschool Activity Book

Trace the lines to each puppy's bed.

Trace the bubbles in the bath.

Trace the candles on the cake.

Aa

Arf

Trace.

Arf

Write.

A

a

Color the shapes with the letters **A** and **a**.

a   H   o   A   a   a   q   D

D   c   a   P   q   A   c   A

B b

Ball

Trace.

Ball

Write.

B

b

Circle B and b.

b B c p g c Q P
p c p G D b G g
D G Q B c B g D
c P B g c g D C
      P   d

Help the puppy swim to the other side of the pond.

Puppy Preschool Activity Book

© Scholastic Inc.

Draw a line from each puppy to its mother.

1

Trace.

Write.

Color the shapes with the number 1.

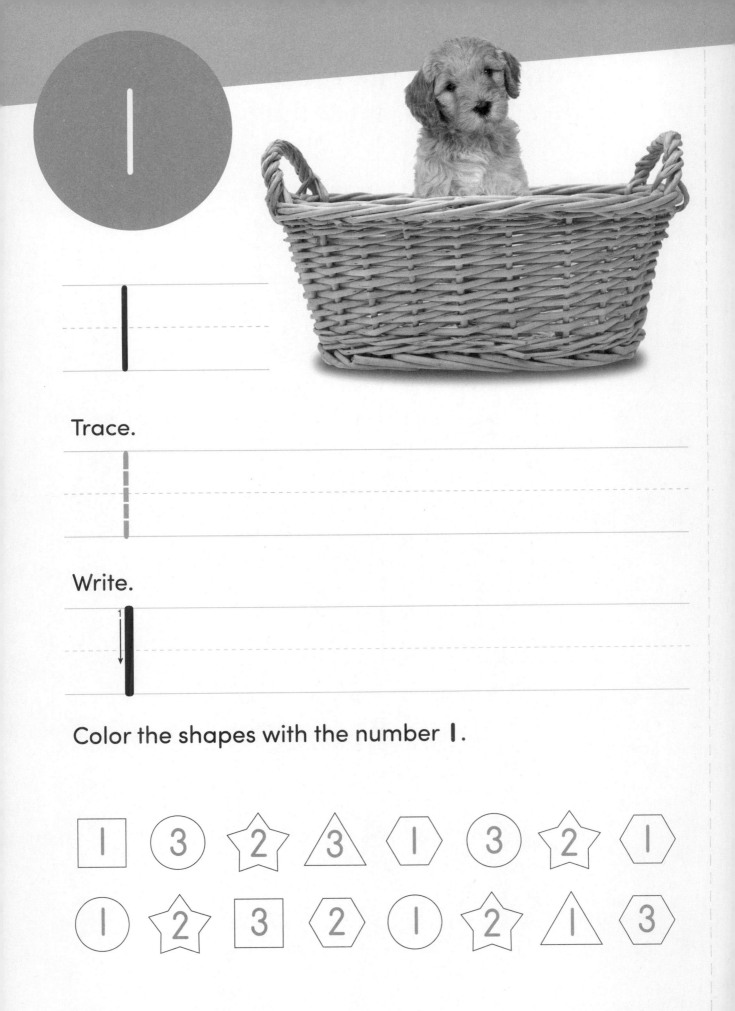

Find each 1. Color that space  RED
Then color the rest of the picture.

Draw a bed for the puppy.

Cut out the puzzle pieces. Use them to make a puppy! Paste the pieces in the frame.

Circle **5** differences.

Cc

Collar

Trace.

Collar

Write.

C

c

Write **c** to complete each word.

 at  up

Dd

Dog

Trace.

Dog

Write.

D

d

Color the pictures that begin with **D**.

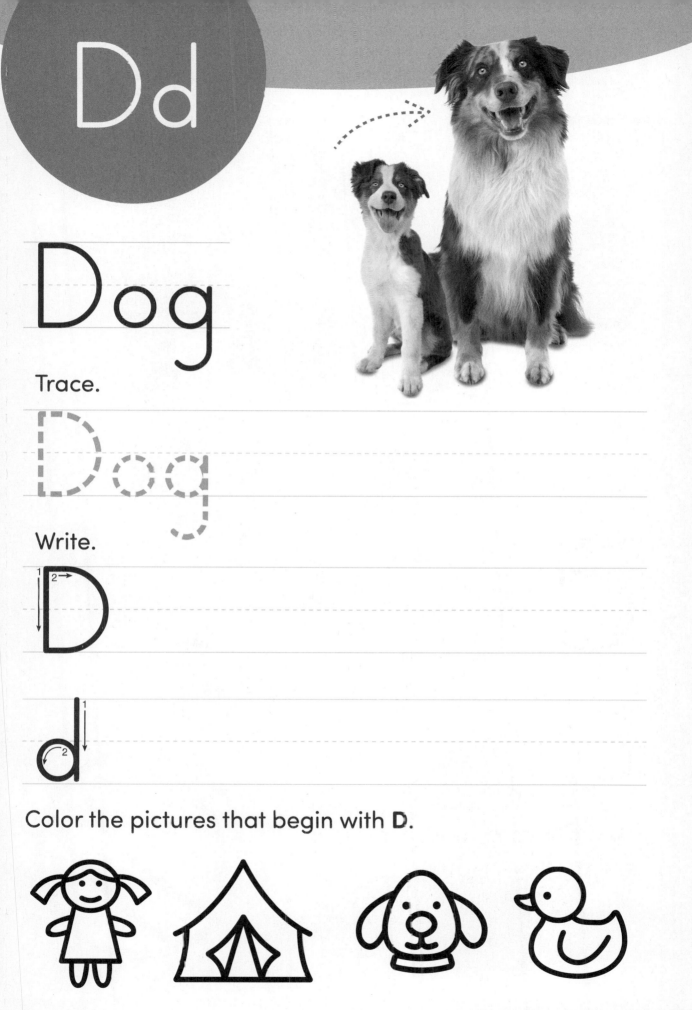

Red

Circle the things that are **red**.

Color the ball RED.

Circle the puppy that is in **front** of the plant.

Circle the puppy that is **behind** the shoe.

2

2

Trace.

2

Write.

2

Circle each 2.

2 1 3 2 1 3 1 3 3 1
3 2 1 3 2 3 2 1 2
1 2 3 3 2 3 2 1 3

Circle the things that come in 2's.

Color the picture. Use the color key.

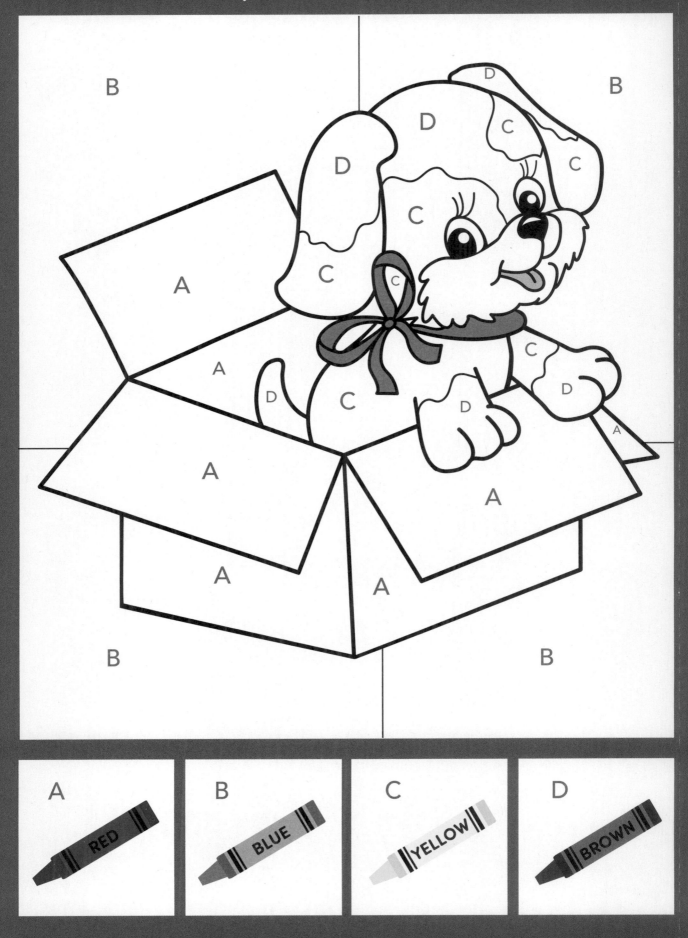

A — RED
B — BLUE
C — YELLOW
D — BROWN

Cut out the lowercase letters. Paste each next to its matching uppercase letter.

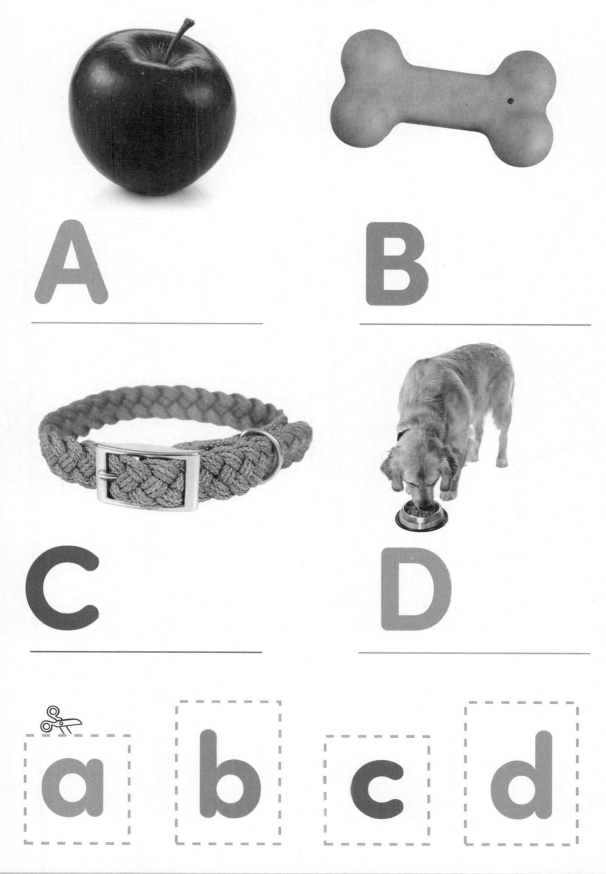

A

B

C

D

a b c d

Trace the circle and the square.

square

circle

Color the circles **red**. Color the squares yellow.

E e

Ear

Trace.

Ear

Write.

E

e

Trace the puppy's ears. Write e on each ear.

Ff

Fluffy

Trace.

Fluffy

Write.

F

f

Circle the treats with the letters **F** and **f**.

Help the puppy find the toys.

Circle the picture that is **different** in each set.

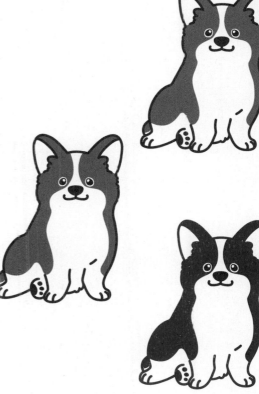

3

3

3

3

Draw **3** balls for the puppy to play with.

Draw **3** spots on the puppy.

Count the puppies. Write the number.

Cut out the pictures. Paste the correct number of dogs in each space below.

1

2

3

Circle 5 differences.

Gg

Groom

Trace.

Groom

Write.

G

g

Color each toy that has **G**.

Hh

LET'S PLAY!

Howl

Trace.

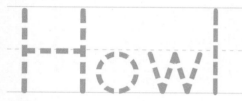

Write.

H

h

Color the shapes with the letters **H** and **h**.

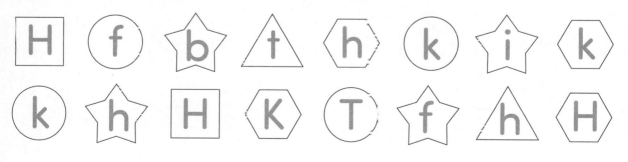

Yellow

Circle the things that are yellow.

Color the puppy's bed YELLOW.

What comes next? Draw it!

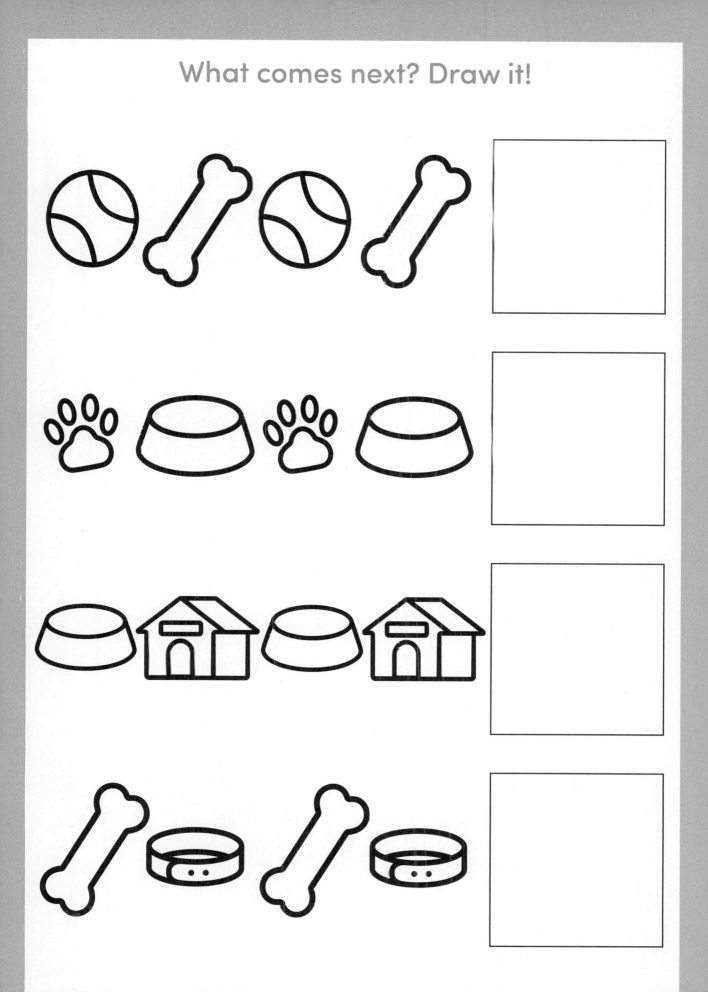

4

4

Trace.

4

Write.

Write the missing numbers.

Draw **4** treats in the puppy's bowl.

Connect each balloon to the puppy with the matching lowercase letter.

Cut out the puppy pictures. Paste them in order of size from smallest to largest.

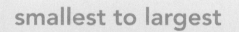

smallest to largest

Find and circle these items in the big picture.

I i

Itch

Trace.

Itch

Write.

2→
1
↓
3→

2•
1↓
i

Circle **I** and **i**.

i t I f L I c T P
T I J J i T L T
I J P J J t J J I t
J P J J I L
J t J L t

Jj

Jog

Trace.

Jog

Write.

J

j

Write **j** to complete each word.

___acket

___ump

Help the puppy find its mother.

Match each number to a set.

2

4

1

3

5

5

Trace.

5

Write.

5

Color **5** stars on the puppy carrier.

Count the puppy toys in each set.
Circle the number.

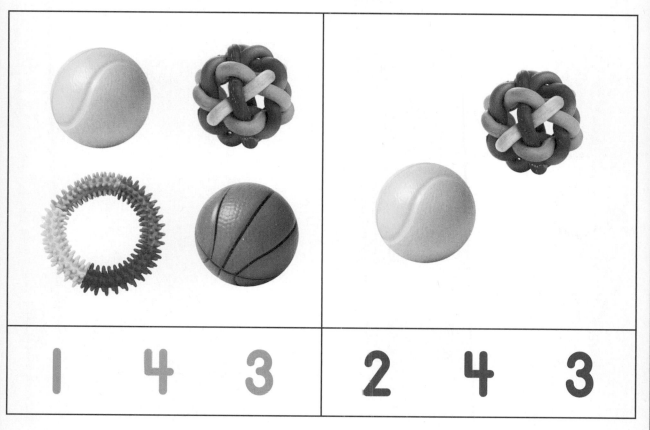

| 1 | 4 | 3 | 2 | 4 | 3 |

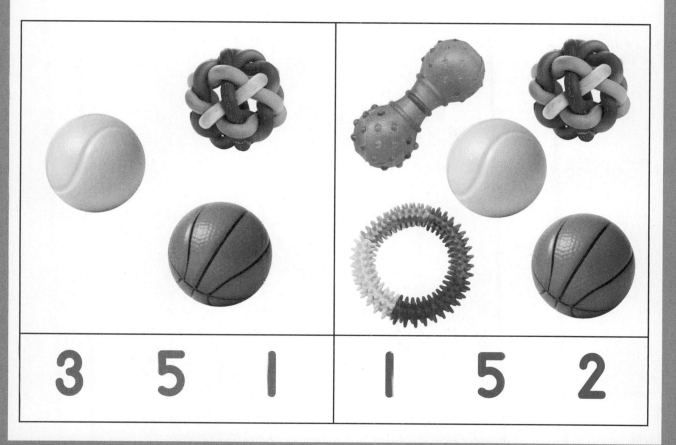

| 3 | 5 | 1 | 1 | 5 | 2 |

In each set, circle the puppy with **more** toys.

Cut out the pictures below.
Use them to complete each pattern.

Circle **5** differences.

Kk

Kid

Trace.

Kid

Write.

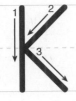

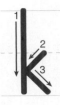

Color the pictures that begin with **k**.

Ll

Lick

Trace.

Lick

Write.

L

l

Write **l** on each bowl.

Blue

Circle the things that are blue.

Color the bowls BLUE.

Circle the two puppies that are **big**.

Circle the two puppies that are **small**.

Connect the dots from 1 to 10.
Then color the picture.

Count the puppies. Write the number.

Write the missing letters in each row.

A C

E H

J L

Cut out the numbers. Paste each next to the set with the same number of treats.

Trace the rectangle and the triangle.

rectangle

triangle

Color the rectangles green.
Color the triangles blue.

Mm

Mud

Trace.

Mud

Write.

m

Circle the name tags with the letters M and m.

Nn

Nap

Trace.

Nap

Write.

N

n

Color each bed that has N.

Help the puppy find its friends.

Puppy Preschool Activity Book

Count each type of puppy.
Color one box in the graph for each puppy.

	1	2	3	4
	1	2	3	4
	1	2	3	4
	1	2	3	4

6

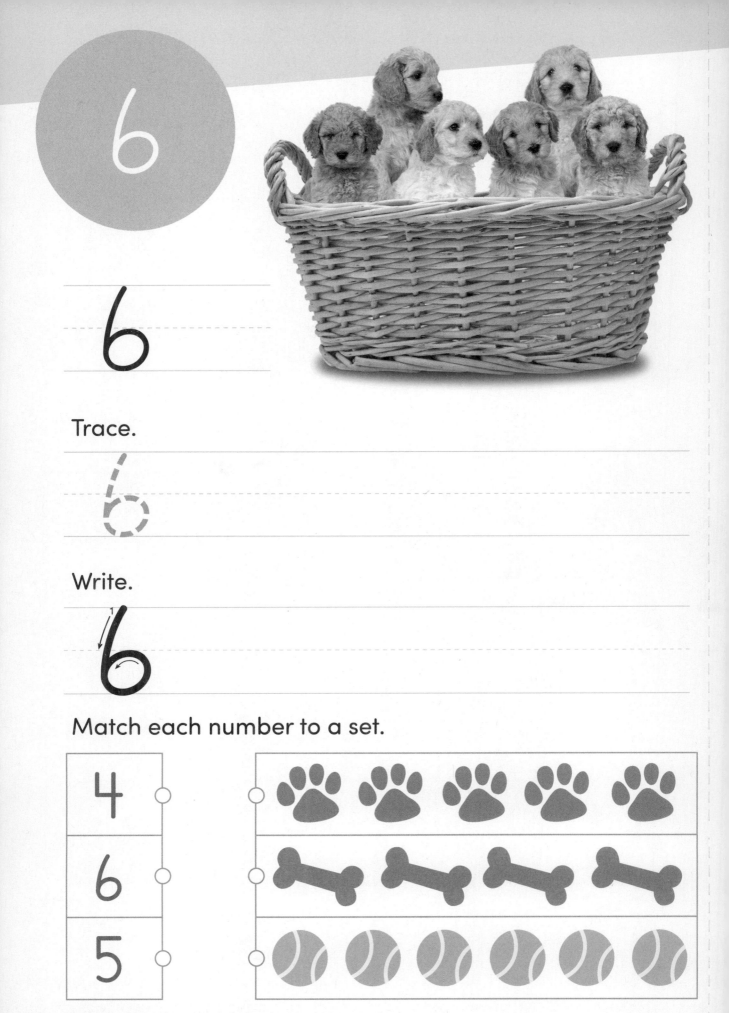

Trace.

6

Write.

6

Match each number to a set.

| 4 |
| 6 |
| 5 |

Circle the things that come in 6's.

In each set, circle the puppy with **fewer** toys.

Circle **5** differences.

Connect the dots from A to N.
Then color the picture.

Cut out the uppercase letters. Paste each next to its matching lowercase letter.

e f h

m n l

E F H M N L

Draw **6** stripes on the puppy's winter coat.

Oo

Oops

Trace.

Oops

Write.

O

o

Color the paw prints with the letters **O** and **o**.

Puppy Preschool Activity Book

P p

Paw

Trace.

Paw

Write.

P

p

Circle **P** and **p**.

b o B D d d p O P
o o F O p f b D b B F
P F O B o d B d p
b b P B o o d d o b

Green

Circle the things that are green.

Color the puppy's harness GREEN.

What comes next? Draw it!

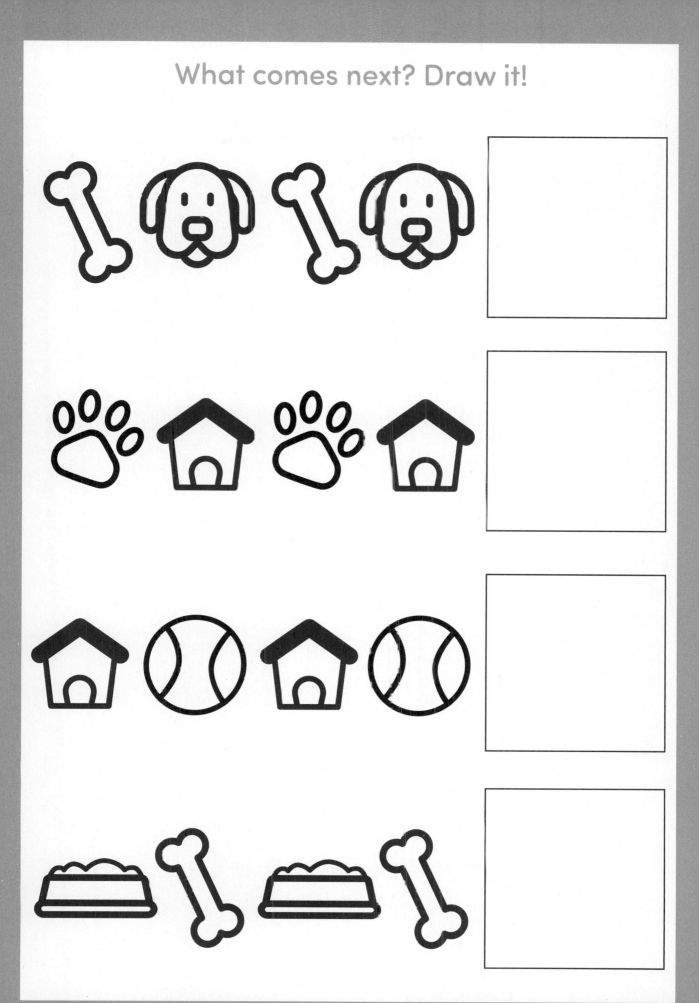

7

Trace.

Write.

Color the shapes with the number **7**.

7   6   5   7   6   5   7   7

5   6   7   6   5   7   5   6

Find each 7. Color that space BLUE.
Then color the rest of the picture.

Find and circle these items in the big picture.

Cut out the labels. Paste them next to each part of the puppy.

mouth　eye　tail　paw

tongue　nose　fur　ear

Name each picture. What beginning sound does each make? Circle it.

M   N   H

C   P   O

P   B   D

M   W   N

Qq

Queen

Trace.

Queen

Write.

Q

q

Write **q** on each box.

_____   _____   _____

Rr

Run

Trace.

Run

Write.

R

r

Color the pictures that begin with **R**.

Help the puppy find the treats.

Match each puppy to a shadow.

8

8

Trace.

Write.

Circle each group of **8**.

Circle the things that come in 8's.

Say each number.
Circle that many puppies in each set.

6	
8	
5	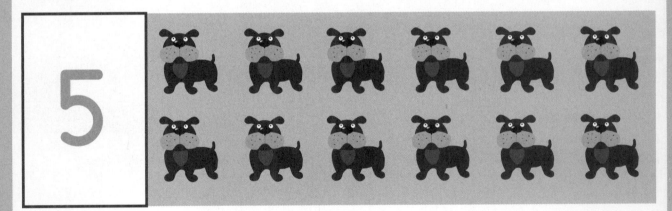
7	

Cut out the shapes.
Paste them where they belong in the picture.

FIRE STATION

Circle **5** differences.

S s

Shake

Trace.

Shake

Write.

S

s

Write **S** to complete each word.

_____

wim  tick

Tt

Tail

Trace.

Tail

Write.

2 →
1
T

1 ↓
2 →
t

Circle the balls with the letters **T** and **t**.

t   T   L   t   T

J   f   T   t   J

Orange

Circle the things that are orange.

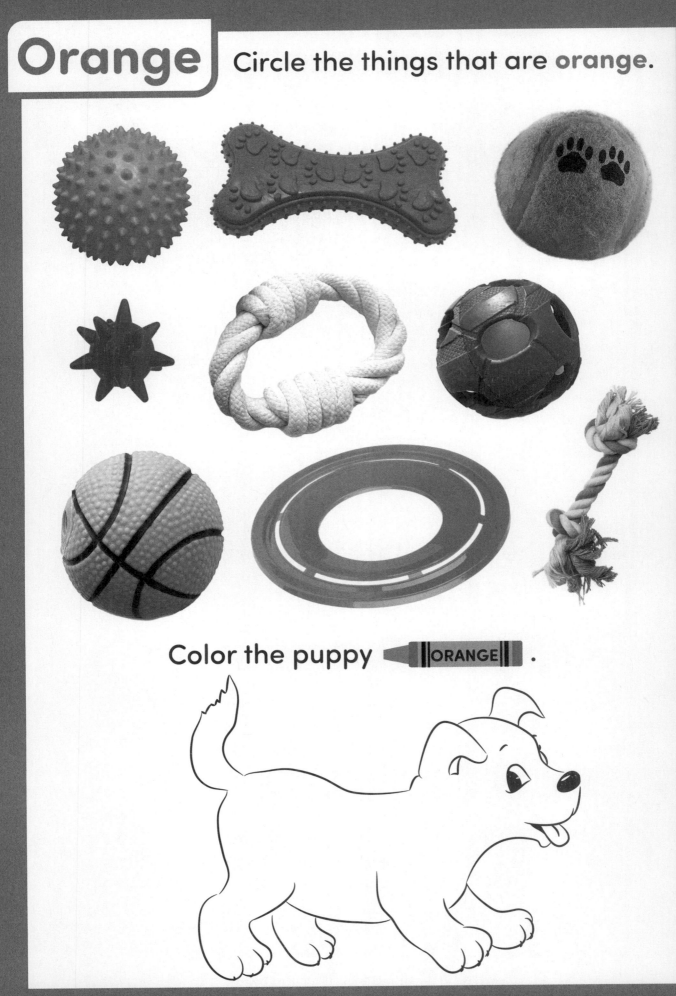

Color the puppy ORANGE .

Circle the puppy that is **in** the box.

Circle the puppy that is **out** of the bucket.

9

9

Trace.

9

Write.

9

Circle each 9.

9 1 3   9 1 3 9
 2   2 3   2   2 2
1 3   9   9   3 1
 9   1   1 3   3   3

Count the puppies in each basket.
Circle the number.

5   8   3

7   6   4

9   4   3

1   4   5

Color the picture. Use the color key.

Q	R	S	T
RED	BLUE	YELLOW	ORANGE

What is missing? Cut out the pictures below. Use them to complete each pattern.

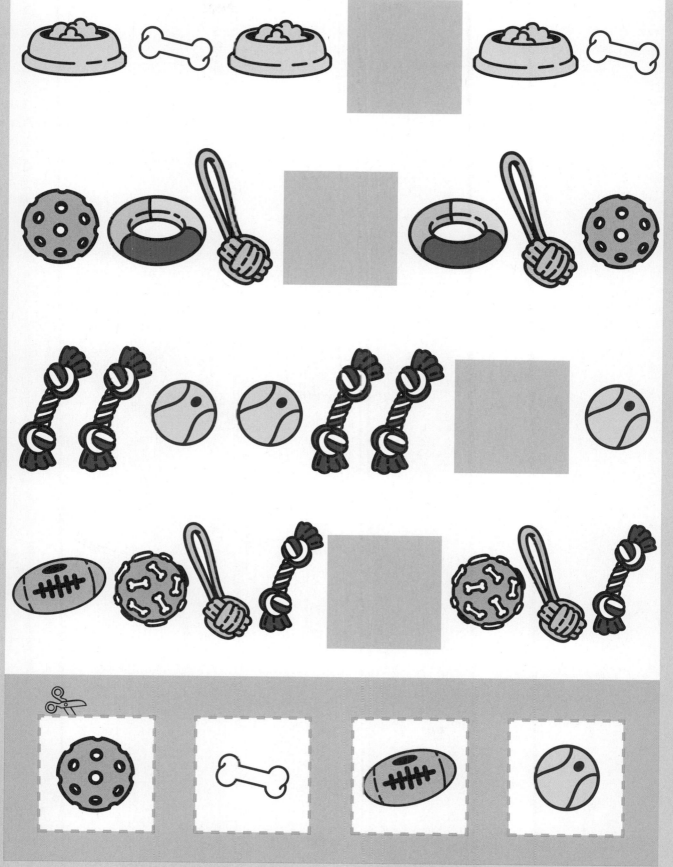

Trace the oval and the diamond.

diamond

oval

Color the ovals **blue**.
Color the diamonds **orange**.

Uu

Under

Trace.

Under

Write.

U

u

Color each toy that has **U**.

© Scholastic Inc.

Vv

Vet

Trace.

Vet

Write.

V

v

Color the shapes with the letters **V** and **v**.

| v | m | u | V | U | U | v | N |

| n | v | M | w | u | W | m | V |

Help the girl find her puppy.

Puppy Preschool Activity Book

© Scholastic Inc.

Count each shape.
Color one box in the graph for each shape.

▬	1	2	3	4
 ▲	1	2	3	4
●	1	2	3	4
■	1	2	3	4
◆	1	2	3	4
⬮	1	2	3	4

10

10

Trace.

Write.

Match each number to a set.

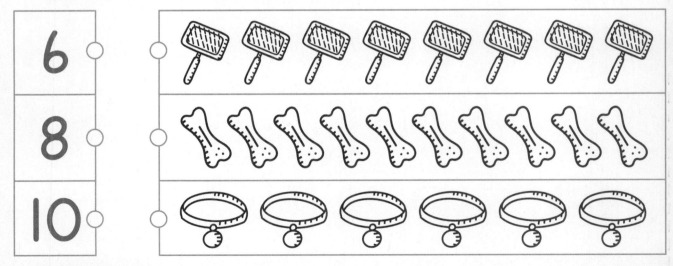

6

8

10

Find and circle 10 🦋 in the picture.

Count the puppies. Write the number.

Cut out the numbers. Paste each next to the set with the same number of dog houses.

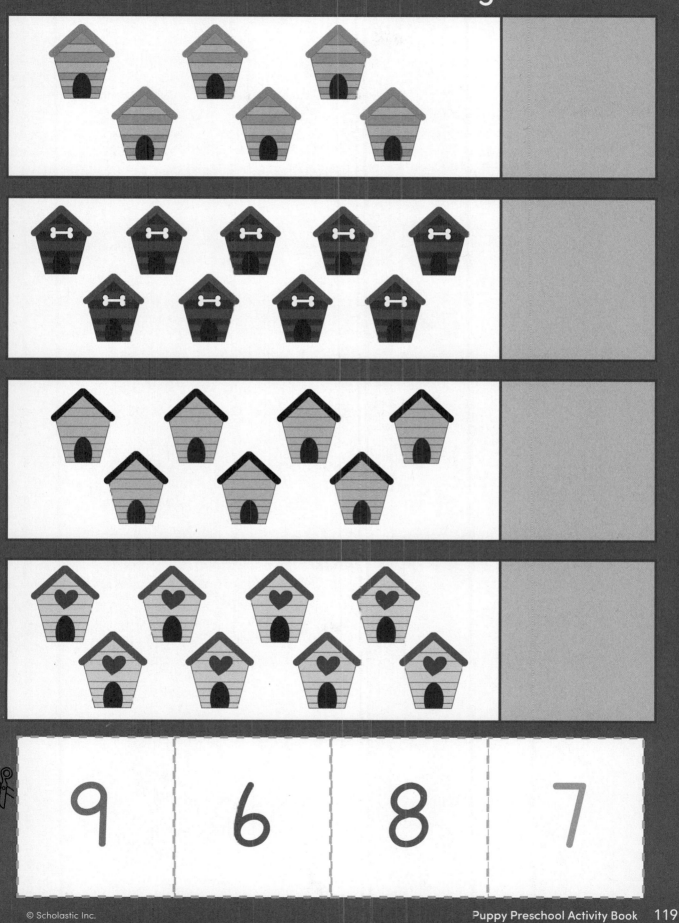

Circle 5 differences.

Ww

Wig

Trace.

Wig

Write.

W

W

Write **W** to complete each word.

___et   ___alk

Xx

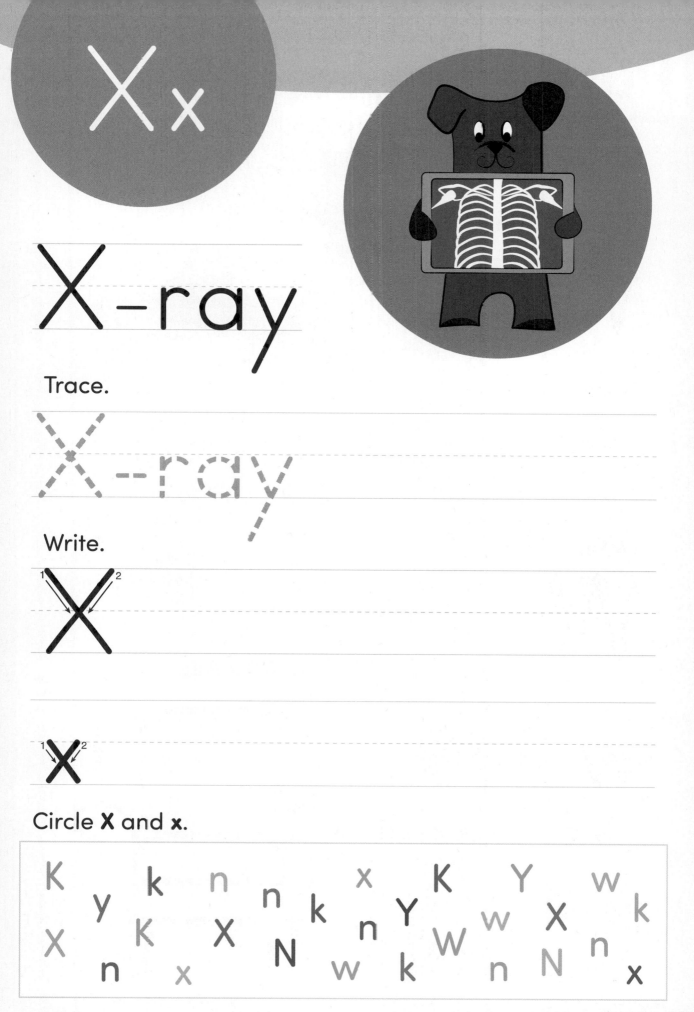

X-ray

Trace.

X-ray

Write.

X

x

Circle X and x.

K Y k n n x K Y w
Y K X n k n Y w X k
X K X N N w X N
n x N w k n N x

Purple

Circle the things that are purple.

Color the chair  PURPLE.

Draw the missing shape.

Connect the dots from 1 to 10.
Then color the picture.

Color the picture. Use the color key.

Color Key

Red   Yellow   Green   Orange   Purple   Blue

Write the missing letters.

b c e

g h j

l m o

p r t

u w x

y

Cut out the puppy pictures.
Paste them in the park.

Find and circle these items in the big picture.

Yy

Yawn

Trace.

Yawn

Write.

Y

y

Color each toy that has **Y**.

Zz

Zzzz

Zzz

Trace.

Zzz

Write.

1 → 2
Z
3 →

1 → 2
Z
3 →

Write **z** on each triangle. Write **Z** on each circle.

Help the puppy find the firefighter.

Match each puppy to its twin.

In each set, circle the puppy with **more** toys.

Draw 10 spots on the puppy.

Circle the puppy that is **on** the table.

Circle the puppy that is **below** the cloud.

What letters are missing? Cut out the letters below. Paste each where it belongs.

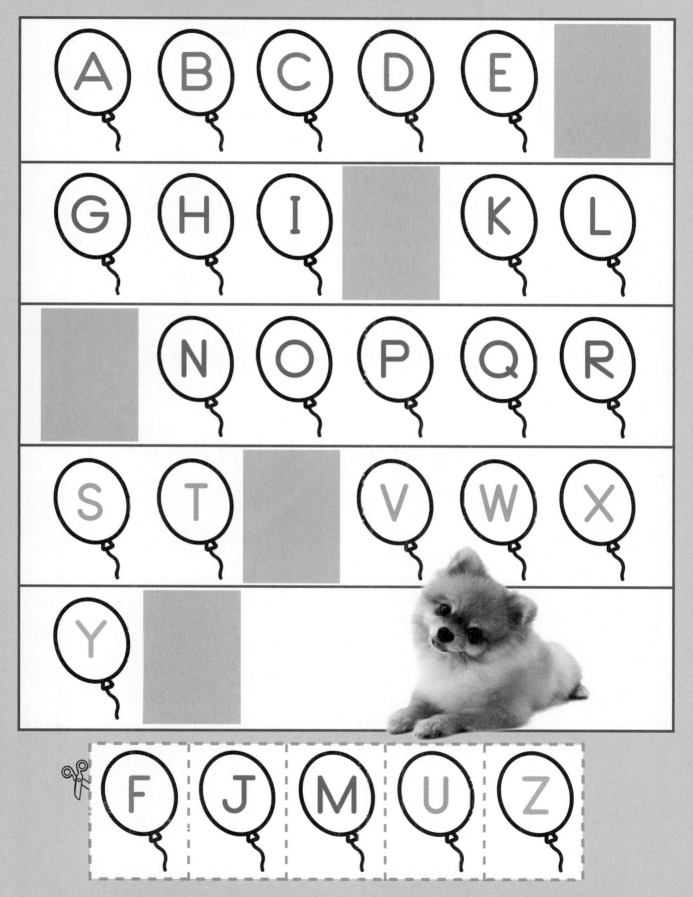

A B C D E ___

G H I ___ K L

___ N O P Q R

S T ___ V W X

Y ___

F J M U Z

Connect the dots from A to Z.
Then color the picture.

Circle **5** differences.

Circle **5** differences.

Find and circle these items in the big picture.

Circle **5** differences.

Circle **5** differences.

Find and circle these items in the big picture.

Circle **5** differences.

Circle **5** differences.

Find and circle these items in the big picture.

CONGRATULATIONS!

This certificate is awarded to

FOR OUTSTANDING ACHIEVEMENT

Signed

Date

Printed in the U.S.A. PO# 50758840

Images © Shutterstock Inc. • 717881